ST

To be a Christian, first and foremost is to love and respect fellow human beings and through this love to come closer to God. Saints on earth and in heaven help us to try to do this by the example they give us. Even during his lifetime it was quite clear that St David was a very special person...

1

The Viking raids all but finished St Davids. Tradition records that it lay waste for seven years before the Christian community returned. St Davids was rebuilt on a sheltered site on either side of the River Alun and soon pilgrims were coming from all over Wales to pray at St David's shrine. . .

'THE CLOSE' INSIDE THE FENCE

'CELLS' FOR THE MONKS

STONE CROSSES

GRAVE YARD

CHURCHES

ST DAVIDS ABOUT 1000

FINE, COLOURFUL 'ILLUMINATED MANUSCRIPTS' WERE MADE

VITA

BUT THERE WAS A MORE SINISTER PILGRIM ON THE WAY

1081

IT'S KING WILLIAM..THE CONQUEROR

ST DAVID, PRAY FOR US

HMM..THE FARMS AND HARBOURS ARE GOOD ROUND HERE

ST DAVID'S REMAINS WERE KEPT IN A SHRINE

CARDIGAN

RHYDYGORS

ST DAVIDS

PEMBROKE

SWANSEA

CARDIFF

TO IRELAND

THE NORMANS HAD COME TO STAY!

FROM NOW ON BISHOPS WERE APPOINTED BY THE KING

BISHOP BERNARD 1115

2

WHAT IS A BISHOP?

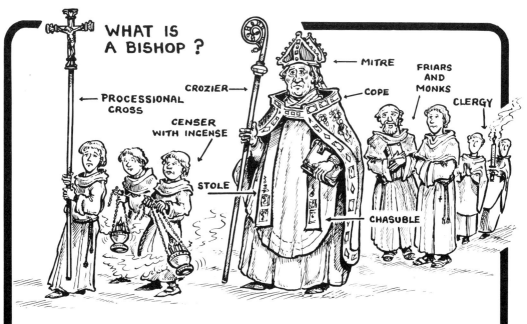

PROCESSIONAL CROSS

CENSER WITH INCENSE

CROZIER

MITRE

COPE

FRIARS AND MONKS

CLERGY

STOLE

CHASUBLE

A bishop is an overseer of the work and welfare of the clergymen within his diocese. It is an ancient office, going back (according to tradition) to the time of St Peter who is remembered as the first bishop of Rome. He is often portrayed holding two keys: one to open the door into a person's soul and the other to unlock the gates of the kingdom of heaven. To this day the two keys of St Peter are the symbol of a bishop. Inside the main church of the diocese, a special chair was set aside for the bishop — *cathedra* in Latin — and this is why such a church is called *cathedral*. Over the centuries, the responsibilities of a bishop have grown and continue to increase. A bishop is first of all concerned with the spiritual welfare of the Christians in his diocese. He is concerned with the physical well-being of the people, clergy and others, who work in the diocese and also the churches, lands, and buildings belonging to the diocese.

CATHEDRA

STATE DUTIES IN PARLIAMENT

4

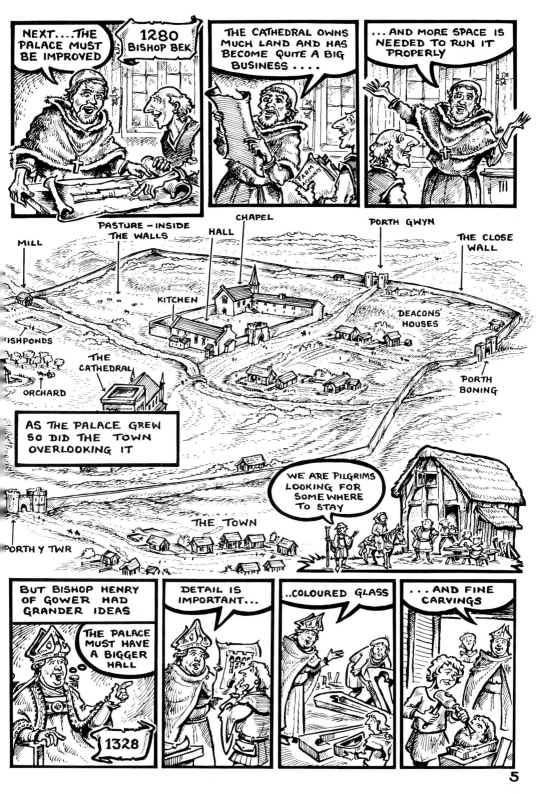

5

THE PALACE IN ITS HEYDAY AT ABOUT 1400

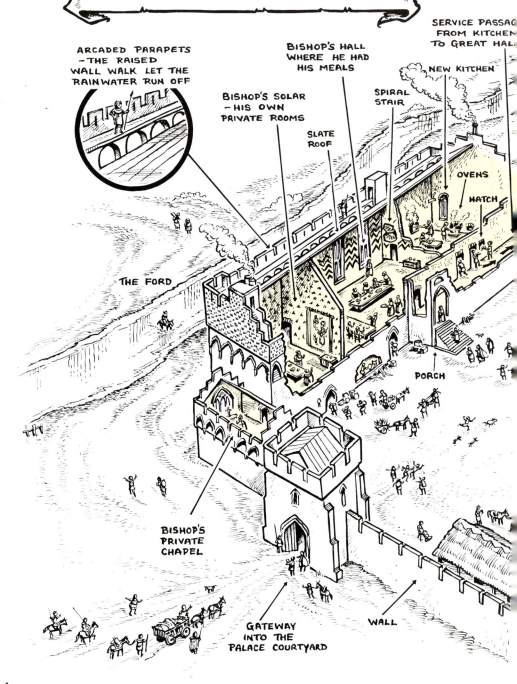

ARCADED PARAPETS – THE RAISED WALL WALK LET THE RAINWATER RUN OFF

BISHOP'S SOLAR – HIS OWN PRIVATE ROOMS

BISHOP'S HALL WHERE HE HAD HIS MEALS

SLATE ROOF

SPIRAL STAIR

SERVICE PASSAGE FROM KITCHEN TO GREAT HALL

NEW KITCHEN

OVENS

HATCH

THE FORD

PORCH

BISHOP'S PRIVATE CHAPEL

GATEWAY INTO THE PALACE COURTYARD

WALL

'CLOSE' WALL

FISHPOND

MILL

WHEEL WINDOW

RIVER ALUN

GALLERY

SCREENS

LEAD ROOF

THE GREAT HALL —WAS USED FOR SPECIAL OCCASIONS AND VISITORS

BELL-COTE

PORCH

CHAPEL

BARREL VAULTS —FOR STORAGE UNDER THE MAIN BUILDING

VESTRY

GUEST ROOMS

LET'S SEE WHAT LIFE WAS LIKE IN THE PALACE

As we have seen, bishops became powerful men and lived in a style appropriate to their status. They played an active part in affairs of state (and still do), so the palace was not just a fine house to live in, it was also a place of work — and 'work' could sometimes be entertaining guests to dinner!

9

The Church was given land to provide food and money for its upkeep. In this way, the bishops became responsible for running great estates.